D1562596

How to Make
a
Boy or Girl Baby!

Also by Shelly Lavigne

BOY OR GIRL?
50 Fun Ways to Find Out

How to Make a Boy or Girl Baby!

61 Old Wives' Tales for Determining the Sex of Your Next Child

by
Shelly Lavigne

Illustrated by Kimbel Mead

A Dell Trade Paperback

A DELL TRADE PAPERBACK

Published by
Dell Publishing
a division of
Bantam Doubleday Dell Publishing Group, Inc.
1540 Broadway
New York, New York 10036

Library of Congress Cataloging in Publication Data
Lavigne, Shelly.
How to make a boy or girl baby! : 61 old wives' tales for determining the sex of your next child / by Shelly Lavigne.
        p.   cm.
ISBN: 0-440-50709-X
1. Pregnancy—Folklore.   2. Sex preselection—Folklore.   3. Infants—Folklore.
I. Title.
GR450.L39 1996   95-43832
398.27—dc20   CIP

Printed in the United States of America
Published simultaneously in Canada
Book design by Susan Maksuta
August 1996

10 9 8 7 6 5 4 3 2 1

FFG

Contents

Introduction

Introduction

My first book, *Boy or Girl?*, is a collection of old wives' tales on how to predict whether you will have a boy or girl when you're pregnant. I interviewed many people to collect my tales, and would often be asked the same question: "How about telling me how to have a girl next time . . . I've got two boys . . . do you know anything about that?!"

I could see that this was a very popular subject, so I started to ask people if they knew any tales dealing with how to conceive a boy or girl. The result is a collection of some pretty funny—and certainly not very scientific—tales. So here they are . . . GOOD LUCK!

§⪑

Chapter One

Your Wedding Night

Wives' tales have suggested for years that what you do on your wedding night can determine the sex of your baby-to-come.
If it's too late for you to use these wedding-night tactics, how about passing them on to someone who's about to tie the knot!

Don't Hold the Garlic . . .

Lots of old wives swear that hanging a garlic bud from your bedpost on your wedding night guarantees your firstborn will be a baby girl.

Pass the Salt

A Romanian tale tells us if you're looking forward to a baby dressed in blue—better sprinkle salt in your bed.

Hail the Veil

Don't pack that veil away on your wedding night! Place it at the foot of your bed (on top of the covers—not under) for a blue bundle of joy.

Hoping for a little bundle in pink? Be sure to place your veil next to your pillow on your wedding night!

4

With This Ring

Newlywed wives are most reluctant to remove their wedding rings. But this tale tells you to place your wedding ring on the floor on your wedding night. Both bride and groom need to step over, but not on, the ring for that boy-to-be.

If it's a girl you're hoping for, the bride should place her wedding ring under the groom's pillow on their wedding night.

5

Three's Company

Germans claim that if a young girl sleeps in the bride and groom's room on their wedding night, the couple will go on to conceive a firstborn daughter (this is probably not a very popular method)!

Pre-Wedding-Night Company?

Swedish folklore tells women to take a young boy into bed on the eve of their weddings to help conceive males on the following night (obviously, a very old tale)!

Chapter Two

Bedroom Babies

W hat happens <u>under</u> <u>the</u> <u>bed</u> as well as on the bed can determine if a boy or girl baby will be in your future.

Nailing It Down

This tale reminds us there weren't many female carpenters years ago. It tells you to place a hammer under your bed for that "handy<u>man</u>"-to-be.

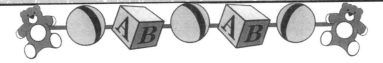

What a Cutup . . .

According to some Danes, placing a pair of scissors under your bed guarantees you'll conceive a precious baby girl.

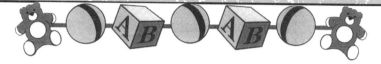

Bow Tied?

If you're wanting to decorate the baby's room in blue, just take a blue ribbon and place it under your pillow.

Place a pink bow underneath your pillow if you're thinking pink!

Stirring It Up

A German tale tells us that placing a wooden spoon under your bed will help you conceive a happy little girl.

A Little Wood Chopper

The Germans also tell us to place an ax under the bed to conceive a baby boy.

13

That's Italian

According to Italians, there's more to ear nibbling than affection. Your husband's nibbles on your left ear encourages a boy conception.

If you prefer a girl, have your husband bite your right ear (tenderly we hope).

I'm So Excited

An old French tale believes that a woman feeling especially amorous during lovemaking will have a son.

No need to get too excited if you're looking to conceive a girl!

Side by Side

Many wives' tales claim if a woman conceives while on her right side, a (not necessarily conservative) baby girl will be born!

Just remember to lie on your left side if you're trying to conceive a (liberal?) little boy.

16

Even, but Not Steven

It's not numerology, just an old wives' tale. If you want a little baby girl, wait to conceive on an even day.

Odd Boy Out

Conceiving on an odd day produces not an "odd" child, but a precious baby boy.

Burning the Midnight Oil

Be sure to check the time on the clock before trying to conceive. Babies conceived before midnight turn out to be timely boys.

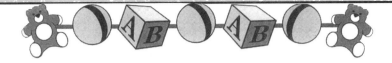

If you're looking to conceive a baby girl, better wait until after midnight.

19

CHAPTER THREE

For the Mom-to-be

Not only are there things mom can do to conceive her little girl or boy, there are things she can just <u>think</u> to make it happen.

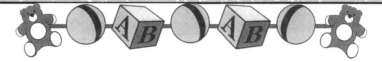

Happy Go Lucky

Little girls are conceived by moms who think happy thoughts, according to an old English tale.

Worry Wart?

Hoping for a little boy? According to the English, just keep on worrying. They believe that little boys are conceived by moms who worry a lot.

22

Dreams Really Do Come True

T his tale has been passed along for years from one German to another. If you dream more often about having a baby boy, your dream will come true.

I f pictures of pink bows and baby girls dominate your dreams, you will conceive a beautiful baby girl.

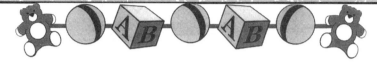

My Place or Yours?

Native Americans will tell you that if you take a small rock from your property and bury it in a wooden box, you will be rewarded with a precious little girl.

And many Native Americans believe that if a small wooden box containing a rock is buried on your <u>neighbor's</u> land, you will conceive a son.

Chapter Four

Eating for Two?

It's been thought for years that what you eat before you try to conceive can influence whether you will have a boy or girl baby.

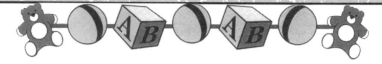

Sugar and Spice

It's no secret that a diet high in sugar and low in salt helps you to conceive that sweet little girl.

Load up on salty pretzels and chips if you wish for a baby boy.

28

Peanuts—Hold the Popcorn

An Irish tale suggests that eating peanuts before conceiving increases your chances of making a son (or going to work for the circus).

Meat and Potatoes

No need to hold back on red meats if you're trying for that healthy, red-blooded boy.

Italian Dressing

Italians everywhere swear that sharing a small drink of olive oil before conceiving will have you not only make a son, but a fine chef.

However tart it may taste, Italians belicve a swig of vinegar before conception aids in the making of a baby girl.

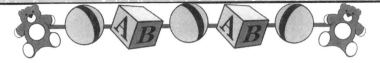

The Juice of the Grape

Before you get ready to make your baby, treat yourself to a glass of grape juice. An old French tale says this encourages the making of a delightful little girl.

Frenchmen believe that a small glass of red wine will help you conceive not a giddy little girl, but a sweet-talking little son.

31

CHAPTER FIVE

Weather Wonders

Rain, sleet, and snow may not deter your mail carrier, but they can affect the arrival of a boy or girl baby. And the moon has its say as well.

That Rainy-Day Feeling

Trying for that little girl? Save it for a rainy day. It's thought that little girls are conceived on rainy days.

High and Dry

A dry sense of humor may be required. It's been told that waiting to conceive during a dry spell will award you with a laughing little boy.

Blowing in the Wind

It's not only farmers who look to the weather. Those hoping to conceive a baby boy should take note of which way the wind is blowing. If it's blowing from the north, you're right on track.

If you're rooting for a pink little bundle, conceiving during a south wind will help you get your wish.

Moon Magic

The moon is the main character in many an old wives' tale. A full moon can make us act a little crazy, but helps you conceive little girls.

Wait to conceive a little boy during a night with a bright quarter moon.

37

By the Light of the Moon

You'll need to check your astrology chart for this one. If the moon is in the sign of Aries, Gemini, Leo, Libra, Sagittarius, or Aquarius at the time of conception, you'll conceive a boy.

If the moon is in Taurus, Cancer, Virgo, Scorpio, Capricorn, or Pisces, a baby girl will be conceived.

CHAPTER SIX

Daddy Dearest

We know that it takes two to conceive, so it's only fair that old wives' tales would give the daddy-to-be some responsibilities too.

Giving It the Boot . . .

Frenchmen say that if your husband places his boots under your bed, a baby girl will be conceived.

Hold On to Your Hat

Some suggest that to make a boy, all Dad needs to do is leave his hat on in bed! Boys are born to hat wearers, you know.

43

Hot Pants

No need to be a "jock," just a guy who wears the right underwear! The word is that wearing Jockey shorts can lead to fathering a little baby girl.

Hanging loose in boxer shorts is for a guy who wants to father "a little guy."

44

The Nose Knows

A Jewish tale tells fathers-to-be to check the mirror. Those with a prominent nose are inclined to father a baby girl.

If Dad's nose is more flat than prominent, he can count on a little baby boy.

45

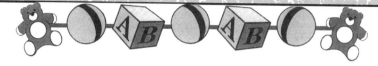

What'll It Be?

An English tale suggests that having a man drink a cup of coffee or tea before "making" your baby perks up the chances for a male baby.

But if dad-to-be slugs down a glass of orange juice, he'll father a sweet little girl.

47

Beefing Up Daddy

If it's a girl you desire, it's time for Dad to get to the club. Norwegians insist that girls are born to dads who build themselves up.

48

Let that gym membership expire if a boy is your wish. No need to work out for a son.

Running Hot and Cold?

This old tale tells men to take a cold shower before "making" your baby. Jumping in a cold shower will produce a frisky little boy.

A hot tub bath warms up the chances for a cuddly baby girl.

50

Heir Raising

Hey—who said being bald is bad? A Polish tale insists bald men produce cute (and sometimes hairy) little boys.

A man with a full head of hair has one more reason to gloat. It's believed he'll make a beautiful baby girl as well.

CHAPTER SEVEN

What About Baby Number Two?

Believe it or not, there are quite a few tales that predict what your next baby will be after your first child. Old wives' tales say it's never too late.

Keep On Hoping . . .

1. If your baby is born with dimples on its legs, your next baby will be a girl.

2. If your first baby has a natural part in the back of his or her head, your next baby will be a boy.

3. If your baby gets teeth very early, your next child will be a boy.

4. If your baby says "Mama" first, your next baby will be a girl.

5. The gender of the first person a woman meets on the way out of the hospital after having a baby will be that of her next child.

54

Happy Endings

L ate one evening, while I was working on this book, I watched a guest being interviewed on a talk show. She was a well-known actress who already had two girls and was expecting her third child. The actress proceeded to tell the host that she knew the sex of the baby she was carrying. There was much anticipation from the crowd, so the actress excitedly announced that they were expecting another daughter. A loud moan came over the audience. "Too bad."

The actress smiled and was taken by surprise. She awkwardly said, "Now, come on, you guys . . . that's okay . . . it's good!"

And it surely is.

Some moms dream of girls and get boys.
Some moms desire boys and get girls.
No matter what, we love each one of you
and wouldn't change you for the world.

To my second precious daughter, Carly.
Love, Mom